The AFTERLIFE

Learn How to Biblically Prepare For It in This Life

Barbara Ann Fields

authorHOUSE®

AuthorHouse™
1663 Liberty Drive
Bloomington, IN 47403
www.authorhouse.com
Phone: 1 (800) 839-8640

Published by AuthorHouse 06/27/2020

ISBN: 978-1-7283-6500-8 (sc)
ISBN: 978-1-7283-6499-5 (e)

Print information available on the last page.

*Any people depicted in stock imagery provided by Getty Images are models,
and such images are being used for illustrative purposes only.
Certain stock imagery © Getty Images.*

*Scripture quotations marked AMP are from The Amplified Bible, Old Testament copyright ©
1965, 1987 by the Zondervan Corporation. The Amplified Bible, New Testament copyright
© 1954, 1958, 1987 by The Lockman Foundation. Used by permission. All rights reserved.*

*All scripture quotations, unless otherwise indicated, are taken
from the King James Version of the Bible.*

This book is printed on acid-free paper.

CONTENTS

DEDICATION

This publication is dedicated to everyone who is serious about their eternal salvation; to everyone who sincerely desires a relationship with the Lord, Jesus Christ; to everyone who knows that the Lord can call them from this earth at any moment in time; to everyone who seeks to make heaven their eternal home.

Please read the following pages with an open and expectant heart, asking God to verify all that is printed within. The Lord Jesus only aligns Himself with the truth. Please read this book over and over again as needed. Be blessed!

[The back page bonus, *THE REVELATION*, is truly a life changing revelation.]

INTRODUCTION

It has been said that there are only two decisions that are vitally important in this life. The decision of who you will marry and the decision of salvation. Marriages don't always work out as they should although the Word of God has strong teachings on the subject. {Matthew 5:32; Matthew 19:3-9; 1 Corinthians 7:1-16; Ephesians 5:22-25; 1 Peter 3:1-7}.

Salvation, however, *must* work out! It involves eternity! The spirit, soul, and new body will have an eternal home. It's up to you to decide where that eternal home will be. Your salvation is not based on what church your parents or grandparents attended or even what church they may have built. That is a carnal, deadly confidence that has nothing to do with spiritual things. The salvation of souls can only be secured through the dictates of the Word of God, {The Bible}, and through obedience to the Word of God. Anything other than God's Word lacks eternal value.

This publication was written and produced by assignment of the Holy Ghost to help prepare souls for the imminent transition of worlds. New Heavens and a New Earth are forthcoming because this *present* world is quickly passing away. {1 Corinthians 7:29-31; 1 John 2:17; Revelation 22:12}. If the population of the current world ever intends to prepare for Jesus' coming, the time is now.

Special Note: Whenever the holy scriptures make a spiritual reference about the heart, the reference concerns the human spirit which is our spiritual heart, not the physical organ in the chest that pumps blood throughout the body.

AFTERLIFE

(Battle Cry!)

While resting, dreaming, and deeply asleep,
the darkness of death craves your soul to reap.

Time cannot forever this life sustain,
sin corrupted humanity's perfect reign.

Today, live righteously before the holy God.
Tomorrow, escape judgment eternal rod.

The flames of hell fail in power through the
second birth, if born again before departing
this earth.

Indeed souls are saved by God's amazing grace.
Yet, only devoted holiness will see His Face.

Stand strong against evil, against all ungodly strife.
Then shall be, for the soul, the inheritance of a glorious
afterlife.

AFTERLIFE

Major Area #1

Never, Ever Forget That This Life Is Temporary!

SCRIPTURES

James 4:13, 14

Go to now, ye that say, to day or to morrow we will go into such a city, and continue there a year, and buy and sell, and get gain: Whereas ye know not what shall be on the morrow. For what is your life? It is even a vapour, that appeareth for a little time, and then vanishest away.

Psalms 103:13-16

Like as a father pitieth his children, so the Lord pitieth them that fear him. For he knoweth our frame; he remembereth that we are dust. As for man, his days are as grass: as a flower of the field, so he flourisheth. For the wind passeth over it, and it is gone; and the place thereof shall know it no more.

1 Peter 1:24

For all flesh is as grass, and all the glory of man as the flower of grass. The grass withereth, and the flower thereof falleth away.

Ecclesiastes 8:8

There is no man that hath power over the spirit to retain the spirit; neither hath he power in the day of death: and there is no discharge in that war......

<u>Notes</u>

Young, old, middle-aged – all races, colors, ethnic groups – rich, poor_........all will pass away. It is appointed unto men once to die.

-Hebrews 9:27

READER'S NOTES

AFTERLIFE

Major Area #2

Remember That Salvation Is Personal

Scriptures

Philippians 2:12

Wherefore, my beloved, as ye have always obeyed, not as in my presence only, but now much more in my absence, work out your own salvation with fear and trembling.

Luke 14:25-27

And there went great multitudes with him: and he turned, and said unto them, If any man come to me, and hate not his father, and mother, and wife, and children, and brethren, and sisters, yea, and his own life also, he cannot be my disciple. And whosoever doth not bear his cross, and come after me, cannot be my disciple.

Notes

Is Jesus telling us to literally hate our relatives? Of course not! Jesus is, however, calling for a total commitment to Him and to the Kingdom of God. This God- commitment will sometimes negatively affect our earthly relationships because it is unlikely that everyone in the family will commit, or submit, to God.

What God requires of us at any given time must be carried out even when family members don't understand it, or when they're against our obedience to God. Again, salvation is personal. One on one – you and Jesus.

Ezekiel 18:20

The soul that sinneth, it shall die. The son shall not bear the iniquity of the father, neither shall the father bear the iniquity of the son: the righteousness of the righteous shall be upon him, and the wickedness of the wicked shall be upon him.

2 Corinthians 5:10

For we must all appear before the judgment seat of Christ; that every one may receive the things done in his body, according to that he hath done, whether it be good or bad.

Notes

The bottom line: *you* are ultimately responsible for *your own* salvation – no pointing fingers at anyone else as to why you didn't give yourself wholly to God.

Matthew 8:21, 22

And another of his disciples said unto him, Lord, suffer me first to go and bury my father. But Jesus said unto him, Follow me; and let the dead bury their dead.

Luke 9:61, 62

And another also said, Lord, I will follow thee; but let me first go bid them farewell, which are at home at my house. And Jesus said unto him, No man, having put his hand to the plough, and looking back, is fit for the Kingdom of God.

<u>Notes</u>

Why were these seemingly reasonable requests condemned by Jesus? Some Bible commentaries tell us that the first man was actually asking for permission to wait until his father died before committing to following Christ. But God will always require that we make Him our first and top priority.

When God brought Elijah into heaven in a chariot of fire, Elisha witnessed it. But Elisha could not go up with Elijah simply based on their relationship/friendship. They each had their own personal relationship with the Lord and God treated them accordingly. 2 Kings 2:1-15

Family, friends, spouses, etc... will not stand before God together, but individually.

Matthew 12:46-50

While he yet talked to the people, behold, his mother and his brethren stood without, desiring to speak with him. Then one said unto him, Behold, thy mother and thy brethren stand without, desiring to speak with thee. But he answered and said unto him that told him, Who is my mother? and who are my brethren? And he stretched forth his hand toward his disciples, and said, Behold my mother and my brethren! For whosoever shall do the will of my Father which is heaven, the same is my brother, and sister, and mother.

READER'S NOTES

AFTERLIFE

Major Area #3

Make Peace With Your Past

Notes

Making peace with your past is two fold. Personal mistakes and failures from your past must, of necessity, be left in the past. Nothing can be done about "all that" now except for you to repent, ask God for His forgiveness, and move forward. God has been handling human failure ever since Adam and Eve failed Him in the Garden of Eden.

Repentance is the first step of salvation for everyone. If there is no turning away from sin, a new life will not be possible. A fresh beginning with God requires a complete break from a dark past.

In relation to the death, burial, and resurrection of Jesus Christ, repentance is our death. Repentance means a **turning away from something**, or to forsake something; it is killing off the old man (old nature); dying to your old way of life to adhere to, and to receive from God a new, vibrant life in Christ.

<u>Scriptures</u>

Colossians 3:9, 10

Lie not one to another, seeing that ye have put off the old man with his deeds; And have put on the new man, which is renewed in knowledge after the image of him that created him.

Mark 1:14, 15

Now after that John was put in prison, Jesus came into Galilee, preaching the gospel of the kingdom of God. And saying, The time is fulfilled, and the kingdom of God is at hand: repent ye, and believe the gospel.

Luke 13:1-5

There were present at that season some that told him of the Galilaeans, whose blood Pilate had mingled with their sacrifices. And Jesus answering said unto them, Suppose ye that these Galilaeans were sinners above all the Galilaeans, because they suffered such things? I tell you, Nay: but, except ye repent, ye shall all likewise perish. Or those eighteen, upon whom the tower in Siloam fell, and slew them, think ye that they were sinners above all men that dwelt in Jerusalem? I tell you, Nay: but, except ye repent, ye shall all likewise perish.

Acts 3:18-21

But those things, which God before had shewed by the mouth of all his prophets, that Christ should suffer, he hath so fulfilled. Repent ye therefore, and be converted, that your sins may be blotted out, when the times of refreshing shall come from the presence of the Lord; And he shall send Jesus Christ, which before was preached unto you: Whom the heaven must receive until the times of restitution of all things, which God hath spoken by the mouth of all his holy prophets since the world began.

Acts 17:29, 30

Forasmuch then as we are the offspring of God, we ought not to think that the Godhead is like unto gold, or silver, or stone, graven by art and man's device. And the times of this ignorance God winked at; but now commandeth all men everywhere to repent.

<u>Notes</u>

It should certainly be known that repentance is not a one-time deal. Life happens. Sin, even that which some people refuse to label as *sin*, can creep in and sometimes take over again. Sin, though, must always be acknowledged and forsaken. An individual overwhelmed by sin needs to seek godly counsel from clergy in order to have his/her spiritual health and equilibrium restored.

The privilege and blessing of repentance, however, must never be abused and used as a plan B for purposeful sinning. Repent, as needed, from sins, mistakes, faults, failures, and shortcomings. Don't fail willfully then use the God-given grace of repentance as a magic wand to cover premeditated acts. People cannot see into the hearts of men, but God certainly can. Synonymous with His Word, God is "a discerner of the thoughts and intents of the heart." Hebrews 4:12d.

Psalms 19:12, 13

Who can understand his errors? cleanse thou me from secret faults. Keep back thy servant also from presumptuous sins; let them not have dominion over me: then shall I be upright, and I shall be innocent from the great transgression.

1 John 1:8, 9

If we say that we have no sin, we deceive ourselves, and the truth is not in us. If we confess our sins, he is faithful and just to forgive us our sins, and to cleanse us from all unrighteousness.

Notes

The past also contains offenses and transgressions committed against us by other people. These offenses, too, must be forgiven and left in the past. Forgiveness of serious transgressions will certainly require time and help from the Lord because real, soul-deep healing does not happen overnight. Still, God does require it. Unforgiveness, unfortunately, will cause many souls to forfeit an afterlife in heaven.

Mark 11:25, 26

And when ye stand praying, forgive, if ye have aught against any: that your Father also which is in heaven may forgive you your trespasses. But if ye do not forgive, neither will your Father which is in heaven forgive your trespasses.

Notes

No one can get into heaven without God's forgiveness of their sins and transgressions. But when we don't forgive others, He cannot forgive us!

Luke 6:36, 37

Be ye therefore merciful, as your Father also is merciful. Judge not, and ye shall not be judged: condemn not, and ye shall not be condemned: forgive, and ye shall be forgiven.

Forgiveness – to release another person(s) from the debt owed; to no longer require payment; to not harbor evil, vengeful thoughts toward someone who has wronged you. Release all to God.

"A refusal to forgive is the same as choosing to carry an unnecessary weight or burden within your soul, making you ineffective in living a life that is happy and victorious."

Matthew 6:12

And forgive us our debts, as we forgive our debtors.

Genesis 50:15-21

And when Joseph's brethren saw that their father was dead, they said, Joseph will peradventure hate us, and will certainly requite us all the evil which we did unto him. And they sent a messenger unto Joseph saying, Thy father did command before he died, saying, So shall ye say unto Joseph, Forgive, I pray thee now, the trespass of thy brethren, and their sin; for they did unto thee evil: and now, we pray thee, forgive the trespass of the servants of the God of thy father. And Joseph wept when they spake unto him. And his brethren also went and fell down before his face, and they said, Behold, we be thy servants. And Joseph said unto them, Fear not: for am I in the place of God? But as for you, ye thought evil against me; but God meant it unto good, to bring to pass, as it is this day, to save much people alive. Now therefore fear ye not: I will nourish you, and your little ones. And he comforted them, and spake kindly unto them.

Psalms 37:8, 9

Cease from anger, and forsake wrath: fret not thyself in any wise to do evil. For evildoers shall be cut off: but those that wait upon the Lord, they shall inherit the earth.

Ephesians 4:31, 32

Let all bitterness, and wrath, and anger, and clamour, and evil speaking, be put away from you, with all malice: And be ye kind one to another, tenderhearted, forgiving one another, even as God for Christ's sake hath forgiven you.

Romans 12:14

Bless them which persecute you: bless, and curse not.

Romans 12:17-21

Recompense to no man evil for evil. Provide things honest in the sight of all men. If it be possible, as much as lieth in you, live peaceably with all men. Dearly beloved, avenge not yourselves, but rather give place unto wrath: for it is written, Vengeance is mine; I will repay, saith the Lord. Therefore if thine enemy hunger, feed him; if he thirst, give him drink: for in so doing thou shalt heap coals of fire on his head.

Notes

Forgiveness is not always easy to practice. The pain of betrayal, violence, and abuse is real; it certainly takes the grace and mercy of the heavenly Father to assist us in releasing that pain to Him. Nonetheless, forgiving others is a God requirement. This subject is not just written about in the Bible to take up space.

Salvation, in and of itself, is indeed a free gift from God through Jesus Christ. Nevertheless, maintaining a healthy relationship with God and with men (the human race), does demand discipline and sacrifice. The lifetime practice of forgiveness is one of those mandatory sacrifices.

READER'S NOTES

_____

_____

_____

_____

_____

_____

_____

_____

_____

_____

_____

_____

_____

_____

_____

_____

_____

_____

_____

_____

_____

_____

_____

_____

_____

_____

_____

_____

_____

AFTERLIFE

Major Area #4

Increase The Size Of Your Inner Circle

(INCREASE YOUR CAPACITY TO LOVE)

Love – This is not always a warm, fuzzy feeling, or a deep affection for an individual; it is erroneous and dangerous to limit love to emotions only. Love is brotherhood and good will toward other people: and it acts accordingly.

Scriptures

Mark 2:15

And it came to pass, that, as Jesus sat at meat in his house, many publicans and sinners sat also together with Jesus and his disciples: for there were many, and they followed him.

Notes

Your group, your friends, your acquaintances, your co-workers, your tight-knit family, your relatives, your neighbors, and so on, are not enough. Everyone needs to expand his/her circle of human fellowship.

This does not mean embracing people who are dangerous, or who indulge in out-of-control behavior. It does mean being open to a wide spectrum of people to advance your personal and spiritual growth and to advance the personal and spiritual growth of others.

Revelation 5:9, 10

And they sung a new song, saying, Thou art worthy to take the book, and to open the seals thereof: for thou wast slain, and hast redeemed us to God by thy blood out of every kindred, and tongue, and people, and nation; And hast made us unto our God kings and priests: and we shall reign on the earth.

Notes

No segregation, elite groups, or 'very important people' (VIP) will exist in Heaven, nor on the New Earth. Jesus came to save *all* people. Your inner circle needs to enlarge more and more. Heaven is too big for small groups and for small minds. The sooner we begin to expand our hearts, minds, and lives to include more people, and different kinds of people, into our personal stratosphere, the sooner we will be prepared for heaven. Our earthly actions and attitudes will follow us into eternity.

1 Samuel 22:1, 2

David therefore departed thence, and escaped to the cave Adullam: and when his brethren and all his father's house heard it, they went down thither to him. And every one that was in distress, and every one that was in debt, and every one that was discontented, gathered themselves unto him; and he became a captain over them: and there were with him about four hundred men.

Notes

David's character drew all types of people to him. David wasn't perfect; no human, in the flesh, is perfect. But David did have a heart of compassion.

We will of course have to ask the Lord to literally give us love for some people who cross our path because there are those who will inspire everything in the heart except love. All of us are acquainted with people who do not exactly make our heart leap with joy when we are around them. God is the only One who can increase our capacity to love. Our efforts of love and goodwill toward men without the God factor involved are most likely superficial. {Besides, we ourselves are not always lovable. Yet, God continues to love us.}

Matthew 5:46, 47

For if ye love them which love you, what reward have ye? do not even the publicans the same? And if ye salute your brethren only, what do ye more than others? do not even the publicans so?

Notes

We may not all fit comfortably into the same social circles, but this does not keep us from indulging in fellowship with different types of people in lines at the grocery stores, at the pharmacies, in the automotive shops, at the hair salons, in the hospitals, in restaurants, etc...... No one knows where, when, or how, new friendships or special relationships will develop.

1 John 4:20

If a man say, I love God, and hateth his brother, he is a liar: for he that loveth not his brother whom he hath seen, how can he love God whom he hath not seen?

1 Corinthians 13:13

And now abideth faith, hope, charity, these three; but the greatest of these is charity.

Notes

We fill our lives with so many things, and with so many activities that are not important to God. "**And he said unto them, Ye are they which justify yourselves before men; but God knoweth your hearts: for that which is highly esteemed among men is abomination in the sight of God**." Luke 16:15 . In the end, despite great human accomplishments, God's question will be, "Did you love people?"

READER'S NOTES

AFTERLIFE

Major Area #5

Baptism Is Not Symbolic; It's A Literal Requirement

Notes

Baptism (in water) is not symbolic in terms of only *representing* a truth. Water baptism is a literal, outward action that solidifies your confession of, your acceptance of, your agreement with, and your identification with Jesus Christ as your Lord and Savior, and as the new Ruler of your life.

Water baptism will probably remain a subject of controversy until the end of time. A sincere individual will need to pray and ask the Lord to impart full understanding and clarity to his/her heart even after this book is read. Please be persuaded by **truth**, not by religion, denomination, popular opinion, or your own intellectual pride.

Scriptures

Romans 6:3-5

Know ye not, that so many of us as were baptized into Jesus Christ were baptized into his death? Therefore we are buried with him by baptism into death: that like as Christ was raised up from the dead by the glory of the Father, even so we also should walk in newness of life. For if we have been planted together in the likeness of his death, we shall be also in the likeness of his resurrection.

Notes

According to the holy scriptures, baptism in water is representative of our burial with Christ. This important step puts us *into* Christ like nothing else can or does. How can anyone be resurrected unless they have first experienced a death and burial? This is what is being explained in Romans, chapter 6.

But an untold number of churches have come away from the 'inconvenience' of potential members having to change out of their clothes, put on clothes appropriate for getting into water, go through the baptism process, and then get dressed all over again. Therefore, some church leaders, because of what is perceived as an outdated hassle, explain away baptism (if it's mentioned at all), as only a symbolic, spiritual element of salvation instead of adhering to a literal immersion in water.

Matthew 3:16

And Jesus, when he was baptized, went up straightway out of the water.

<u>Notes</u>

Jesus always led by example. We cannot choose certain scriptures that we don't mind obeying, then disregard other scriptures that do not line up with our desires or belief system. Since going under water to have your sins washed away is part of the plan of salvation, you need to search out those who will baptize you in water although your current church may not believe in, or teach, the practice of water baptism.

Mark 16:16

He that believeth and is baptized shall be saved; but he that believeth not shall be damned.

<u>Notes</u>

Sprinkling water over a baby's head in the name of a baptism is fine for whatever personal ritual someone desires to acknowledge. However, for the purpose of salvation, an authentic water baptism is performed by a complete submersion.

Acts 8:35-39

Then Philip opened his mouth, and began at the same scripture, and preached unto him Jesus. And as they went on their way, they came unto a certain water: and the eunuch said, See, here is water; what doth hinder me to be baptized? And Philip said, If thou believest with all thine heart, thou mayest. And he answered and said, I believe that Jesus Christ is the Son of God. And he commanded the chariot to stand still: and they went down both into the water, both Philip and the eunuch; and he baptized him. And when they were come up out of the water, the Spirit of the Lord caught away Philip, that the eunuch saw him no more: and he went on his way rejoicing.

Notes

Bodies that are not cremated are placed under the earth, or put away from sight in a tomb, crypt, or mausoleum. Burials are underground. Just as bodies are put under the earth when they die, bodies must be put under water during baptism as a symbol of death and burial. We repent (die out) to sin, and are baptized (buried) as a result of that death to sin, then we rise to walk in a "newness of life" (resurrection).

Notes

In an effort to downplay the need for, or at least the importance of baptism, some people, even some prominent television preachers, gleefully grab onto the declaration made by Paul in 1 Corinthians 1:17a . "For Christ sent me not to baptize, but to preach the gospel." Unfortunately, they do not allow other scriptures to put flesh on the bare bones of Paul's statement.

John 4:1-3

When therefore the Lord knew how the Pharisees had heard that Jesus made and baptized more disciples than John, (Though Jesus himself baptized not, but his disciples,) He left Judea, and departed again into Galilee.

Notes

Paul, like Jesus, had followers or disciples. Paul's focus was preaching the gospel message. He assigned the task of water baptism, along with other ministerial responsibilities, to his helpers.

The pastors in local churches have deacons under their leadership to carry out certain jobs in the church to enable the pastor to give his attention to matters that can only be handled by the pastoral office. Paul is therefore not dismissing baptism and its necessity in the plan of salvation;

he is warning the Corinthians against esteeming the ministers of Christ instead of esteeming Christ only. 1 Corinthians 1:9-17 needs to be read in order to understand the full scope of Paul's reprimand.

Other scriptures that speak to the importance of water baptism are: John 3:5; 1 Corinthians 10:1, 2; Galatians 3:27; Colossians 2:12. In John 3:5, this water birth is not in reference to the natural breaking of a woman's water during the natural human birth process. That explanation is just another secular view against the truth of the holy scriptures.

1 Peter 3:20, 21

Which sometime were disobedient, when once the longsuffering of God waited in the days of Noah, while the ark was a-preparing, wherein few, that is, eight souls were saved by water. The like figure whereunto even baptism doth also now save us (not the putting away of the filth of the flesh, but the answer of a good conscience toward God,) by the resurrection of Jesus Christ.

Notes

Baptism does not cleanse our bodies, nor does it eradicate the human tendency toward wrong doing which became inherent in human nature when Adam and Eve failed in the Garden of Eden. The baptism in water eliminates our consciousness of past sins, clearing the way for a fresh start in Christ and with Christ. The water baptism cleanses our souls! What power! What grace! The promise of a clean and clear conscience should have everyone urgently seeking to be baptized in water, not fighting against it!

The Importance of Baptizing in Jesus' Name

Countless arguments are made in secular Christianity about *how* to baptize, if at all, and about what Name, if any, is to be used during the literal baptism. This subject is not about splitting hairs over trivial matters; it concerns salvation, the most essential aspect of man's existence. The Word of God, of course, is always our final authority.

Acts 2:38a

Then Peter said unto them, Repent, and be baptized every one of you in the name of Jesus Christ for the remission of sins.

Notes

The book of Acts is the beginning of the New Testament Church. It details the many water baptisms that were performed. We've already noted that the eunuch was baptized in the 8th chapter of Acts. In the 10th chapter of Acts, the household of Cornelius was baptized. The 16th chapter tells of Lydia, a seller of purple, who was baptized. Paul and Silas were thrown into prison in that same chapter but the keeper of the prison was soon baptized along with his household. In the 19th chapter of Acts, Paul found disciples that had been baptized by John the Baptist.

Acts 19:4, 5

Then said Paul, John verily baptized with the baptism of repentance, saying unto the people, that they should believe on him which should come after him, that is, on Christ Jesus. When they heard this, they were baptized in the name of the Lord.

Notes

These disciples were baptized *again*, although John the Baptist had baptized them already. Why? God sent John to baptize to prepare the hearts and minds of the people to receive the One coming after John, which was Christ, the Lord.

When Paul met these disciples, Jesus had already returned to heaven; Jesus' earthly mission was fulfilled. The New Testament Church was in full operation at the time Paul came in contact with these certain disciples. Then, as now, all souls are required to be baptized in the "Name of the Lord Jesus Christ".

The <u>Name</u> of Jesus invoked, or said during a baptism is what remits, or removes, sins. (Not the water itself). One argument is that Peter only meant that we are to simply use the ***authority*** of Jesus' name when baptizing and not Jesus' actual name. Paul's teaching, along with other scriptures, refute this argument. The person who is baptizing a soul today is biblically instructed to say, "I baptize you in the Name of the Lord Jesus Christ", or "I baptize you in the Name of Jesus Christ", or "I baptize you in the Name of the Lord, for the remission of your sins."

1 Corinthians 1:12-15

Now this I say, that every one of you saith, I am of Paul; and I of Apollos; and I of Cephas; and I of Christ. Is Christ divided? was Paul crucified for you? Or were ye baptized in the name of Paul? I thank God that I baptized none of you, but Crispus and Gaius: Lest any should say that I had baptized in mine own name.

Acts 8:16b

Only they were baptized in the name of the Lord Jesus.

Acts 10:47, 48

Can any man forbid water; that these should not be baptized, which have received the Holy Ghost as well as we? And he commanded them to be baptized in the name of the Lord. Then prayed they him to tarry certain days.

Acts 22:12-16

And one Ananias, a devout man according to the law, having a good report of all the Jews which dwelt there, Came unto me, and stood, and said unto me, Brother Saul, receive thy sight. And the same hour I looked up upon him. And he said, The God of our fathers hath chosen thee, that thou shouldest know his will, and see that Just One, and shouldest hear the voice of his mouth. For thou shalt be his witness unto all men of what thou hast seen and heard. And now why tarriest thou? arise, and be baptized, and wash away thy sins, calling on the name of the Lord.

Notes

Let's look at another reason why baptism must be done in the Name of the Lord Jesus. A bride must take on the name of her groom or husband. The Bride of Christ (the Church) must take on the Name of Jesus Christ (the Bridegroom).

John 3:28, 29

Ye yourselves bear me witness, that I said, I am not the Christ, but that I am sent before him. He that hath the bride is the bridegroom: but the friend of the bridegroom, which standeth and heareth him, rejoiceth greatly because of the bridegroom's voice: this my joy therefore is fulfilled.

Mark 2:18-20

And the disciples of John and of the Pharisees used to fast: and they come and say unto him, Why do the disciples of John and of the Pharisees fast, but thy disciples fast not? And Jesus said unto them, Can the children of the bridechamber fast, while the bridegroom is with them? As long as they have the bridegroom with them, they cannot fast. But the days will come, when the bridegroom shall be taken away from them, and then shall they fast in those days.

Matthew 25:10

And while they went to buy, the bridegroom came; and they that were ready went in with him to the marriage: and the door was shut.

Revelation 19:7, 8

Let us be glad and rejoice, and give honour to him: for the marriage of the Lamb is come, and his wife hath made herself ready. And to her was granted that she should be arrayed in fine linen, clean and white: for the fine linen is the righteousness of saints.

Revelation 22:17a

And the Spirit and the bride say, Come.

Notes

We become a part of the Church (Bride) when we take on the Name of the Bridegroom (the Lamb, Jesus) during baptism, just as a bride takes on the name of her husband-to-be during a wedding ceremony.

Notes

All scriptures that concern baptism sum up Matthew 28:19 which says, "Go ye therefore, and teach all nations, baptizing them in the name of the Father, and of the Son, and of the Holy Ghost." The Name of Jesus includes all. "**For there are three that bear record in heaven, the Father, the Word (Jesus, or the Son), and the Holy Ghost: and these three are one.**" 1 John 5:7. [See also John 1:1-14].

Colossians 2:8-10

Beware lest any man spoil you through philosophy and vain deceit, after the tradition of men, after the rudiments of the world, and not after Christ. For in him dwelleth all the fulness of the Godhead bodily. And ye are complete in him, which is the head of all principality and power.

Special Note: There will be those who wonder about the thief on the cross and the fact that he was <u>not</u> baptized.

Hebrews 9:16, 17

For where a testament is, there must also of necessity be the death of the testator. For a testament is of force after men are dead: otherwise it is of no strength at all while the testator liveth.

Special Note: As long as Jesus was alive, the Old Testament was alive. This thief appealed to Jesus for salvation while still under Old Testament law. The law was a law of righteousness. When the thief acknowledged his sinful deeds and believed on God, it was counted unto him for righteousness the same as believing God was counted unto Abraham for righteousness. Therefore, the thief was not under New Testament obligations.

READER'S NOTES

_____

_____

_____

_____

_____

_____

_____

_____

_____

_____

_____

_____

_____

_____

_____

_____

_____

_____

_____

_____

_____

_____

_____

_____

_____

_____

_____

_____

AFTERLIFE

Major Area #6

Receive The Gift Of The Holy Ghost!

<u>Notes</u>

The scriptures also use other Names when making reference to the Holy Ghost. It is the Holy Spirit, the Spirit of Truth, the Promise of the Father, and the Comforter. Whatever Name is used, we must receive the Spirit of Christ. It is not an ***option*** or just a ***second blessing*** as some teach. The Holy Ghost living through believers empowers us against sin, self, and satan. And every human on earth will be troubled by all three of these enemies until his/her last breath.

We must be empowered to fight! Spiritual power requires the Spirit; the human "will power" is a very limited power. Human power alone cannot, and will not, help anyone "withstand in the evil day, and having done all, to stand." Ephesians 6:13b .

Scriptures

Acts 1:4, 5, 8

And, being assembled together with them, commanded them that they should not depart from Jerusalem, but wait for the promise of the Father, which, saith he, ye have heard of me. For John truly baptized with water: but ye shall be baptized with the Holy Ghost not many days hence. (8) But ye shall receive power, after that the Holy Ghost is come upon you: and ye shall be witnesses unto me both in Jerusalem, and in all Judaea, and in Samaria, and unto the uttermost part of the earth.

Notes

Jesus commanded that his disciples wait for the promise, which is the power of the Holy Ghost. It not only gave them power to work miracles, the Holy Ghost also gave them courage to withstand the persecution that was on its way. Flesh, or carnality, will give up when the heat of Christian persecution arises. The Spirit of God rises up in boldness when evil criticism comes against those who come against immorality.

Romans 8:8-14

So then they that are in the flesh cannot please God. But ye are not in the flesh, but in the Spirit, if so be that the Spirit of God dwell in you. Now if any man have not the Spirit of Christ, he is none of his. And if Christ be in you, the body is dead because of sin; but the Spirit is life because of righteousness. But if the Spirit of him that raised up Jesus from the dead dwell in you, he that raised up Christ from the dead shall also quicken your mortal bodies by his Spirit that dwelleth in you. Therefore, brethren, we are debtors, not to the flesh, to live after the flesh. For if ye live after the flesh, ye shall die: but if ye through the Spirit do mortify the deeds of the body, ye shall live. For as many as are led by the Spirit of God, they are the sons of God.

Notes

The Spirit, or the Holy Ghost, cannot live *through* us unless it lives *in* us. We see from the above scriptures that the Holy Ghost will be the agent that activates our resurrection - a spiritual resurrection now, and, in the end of time, a literal resurrection. The Spirit is life; we can't rise again without God's life (Spirit) on the inside of us at the time of resurrection.

The Holy Spirit doesn't automatically take up residence in a person's spirit just because an individual speaks a few words of repentance. Further instructions must be given concerning the receiving of this great blessing!

The people of Israel had insisted that Jesus, the Prince of life, be killed. Peter, on the day of Pentecost, (a Jewish feast day), was telling Israel of their sin of crucifying the Christ. Fearing for the future of their eternal souls, they cried out for help.

Acts 2:37-40

Now when they heard this, they were pricked in their heart, and said unto Peter and to the rest of the apostles, Men and brethren, what shall we do? Then Peter said unto them, Repent, and be baptized every one of you in the name of Jesus Christ for the remission of sins, and ye shall receive the gift of the Holy Ghost. For the promise is unto you, and to your children, and to all that are afar off, even as many as the Lord our God shall call. And with many other words did he testify and exhort, saying, Save yourselves from this untoward generation.

Notes

So many people reject receiving the Holy Ghost because they refuse to "speak with other tongues" based on fear, shame, or unbelief; they do not believe that it is necessary to do so. Nevertheless, when the Holy Ghost enters into an individual's spirit, the Spirit takes over his/her tongue, giving evidence of its Presence.

Acts 2:1-8

And when the day of Pentecost was fully come, they were all with one accord in one place. And suddenly there came a sound from heaven as of a rushing mighty wind, and it filled all the house where they were sitting. And there appeared unto them cloven tongues like as of fire, and it sat upon each of them. And they were all filled with the Holy Ghost, and began to speak with other tongues, as the Spirit gave them utterance. And there were dwelling at Jerusalem Jews, devout men, out of every nation under heaven. Now when this was noised abroad, the multitude came together, and were confounded, because that every man heard them speak in his own language. And they were all amazed and marvelled, saying one to another, Behold, are not all these which speak Galilaeans? And how hear we every man in our own tongue, wherein we were born?

<u>Notes</u>

Speaking with other tongues is the initial sign that you have received the gift of the Holy Ghost; afterwards, speaking with other tongues, or praying in the Spirit, builds up, or edifies, your inner man. "But ye, beloved, building up yourselves on your most holy faith, praying in the Holy Ghost." Jude 1:20.

The **divers kinds of tongues** reported in 1 Corinthians 12:1-11 are listed along with the gifts of the word of wisdom, the word of knowledge, the gifts of healing, and so forth. [the <u>divers kinds of tongues</u> could be "of men and of angels" (1 Corinthians 13:1), qualifying them to be on this list of special gifts.]

However, "speaking with other tongues", as noted in Acts 2:1-8 listed above, refers to speaking the different languages of the earth that you did not formally learn, but are now speaking in the 'tongues' of other nations by the power of the Holy Spirit, your initiation into the faith.

This speaking with other tongues, which alerts the believer that God's Spirit now indwells his/her spirit, is not just for certain denominations. The Bible was written to **all people,** to instruct **all people** unto salvation. Different sects and denominations were created by men, not by God.

Acts 10:43-47

To him give all the prophets witness, that through his name whosoever believeth in him shall receive remission of sins. While Peter yet spake these words, the Holy Ghost fell on all them which heard the word. And they of the circumcision which believed were astonished, as many as came with Peter, because that on the Gentiles also was poured out the gift of the Holy Ghost. For they heard them speak with tongues, and magnify God. Then answered Peter, Can any man forbid water, that these should not be baptized, which have received the Holy Ghost as well as we?

Acts 19:2, 6

He said unto them, Have ye received the Holy Ghost since ye believed? And they said unto him, We have not so much as heard whether there be any Holy Ghost. (6) And when Paul had laid his hands upon them, the Holy Ghost came on them; and they spake with tongues, and prophesied.

Notes

How did Peter and the people that came with him know that the Gentiles had received the Holy Ghost? They heard Cornelius and the rest of the people to whom they ministered, speak with other tongues, the initial sign of the Holy Ghost.

How did Paul know that the disciples that he found in Ephesus had received the gift of the Holy Ghost? He heard them speak with tongues.

Although some people have testified to receiving the Holy Ghost without immediately speaking with other tongues, they admitted that they did eventually speak with other tongues because the Holy Ghost was now present in their spirits and the Holy Ghost *will* speak!

Acts 2:10, 11

Phrygia, and Pamphylia, in Egypt, and in the parts of Libya about Cyrene, and strangers of Rome, Jews and proselytes, Cretes and Arabians, we do hear them speak in our tongues the wonderful works of God.

Notes

Again, these "tongues" that we speak when we first receive the gift of the Holy Ghost are languages of other nations. Do not allow anyone to cause you to miss out on this wonderful gift of God by erroneously teaching the chapters of 1 Corinthians 12 and 14 as reasons, or excuses, not to speak with other tongues.

Read the book of 1 Corinthians, chapter 14, both carefully and prayerfully. Paul is setting in order the disorder that was happening in the Corinthian church. Unbelievers were visiting that particular church but could not understand what was happening in the church service because all of the believers were busy edifying themselves by praying in other tongues and were not speaking plainly. Paul insisted that the believers prophesy (speak with understanding) instead of in other tongues whenever unbelievers were among them so that the whole church could be edified. And if they did speak with other tongues among unbelievers, Paul said that someone had to be in the service to interpret that tongue.

1 Corinthians 14:26

How is it then, brethren? when ye come together, every one of you hath a psalm, hath a doctrine, hath a tongue, hath a revelation, hath an interpretation. Let all things be done unto edifying.

Notes

Another interesting fact to consider is that when the disciples returned to Jerusalem to "wait for the promise of the Father", which was the Holy Ghost, Mary, the mother of Jesus, was among those that waited with the disciples in the upper room. Why? Because Mary was not exempt from the necessity of receiving the Spirit of God! In order to be saved, the person who carried the Saviour in her womb had to also receive the Saviour into her spirit! Yes, the Holy Ghost is for everyone!

How to Receive the Holy Ghost

Simply and sincerely, closing out everything and everyone, begin to worship the Lord with all of your heart, asking Him, and believing Him, to fill you with His wonderful gift of the Holy Ghost.

In order to receive the Holy Ghost, you cannot praise and worship the Lord silently in your heart or in your mind. You have to open your mouth, be vocal in seeking this gift! How will the Spirit of God take over your tongue and cause you to speak in other tongues if you are not using your tongue to praise Him? If it doesn't happen the first time, keep seeking the Lord for the Holy Ghost! It has been promised to you! Acts 2:39.

Others have been in a church service where the Spirit of God was moving in a powerful way and the Holy Ghost fell on them in that atmosphere of worship. It could also happen to you in that manner.

Luke 11:13

If ye then, being evil, know how to give good gifts unto your children: how much more shall your heavenly Father give the Holy Spirit to them that ask him?

Why Romans 10:9, 10 are not Scriptures by Which We Obtain Salvation

Romans 10: 9, 10 are widely accepted as, or known to be, "The Sinner's Prayer". There are variations of "The Sinner's Prayer" that a congregation is instructed to repeat. A pastor, a visiting evangelist, or a television preacher, lead people to say, in one form or another, the following words:

"Lord, please forgive me, a sinner. Please forgive all of my sins and trespasses against You. I'm sorry for my sins. I right now, today, give my heart and my life to You, Jesus. Please come into my heart today and save me. I confess You as my Lord and Savior. I believe that God sent You into the world and that He raised You from the dead. Thank You, Lord, for saving me."

The main reason "The Sinner's Prayer", which is a repeat-after-me salvation, is erroneous is because Romans through Revelation are epistles, or letters, written to the Church of the Living God, not to unbelievers seeking salvation. The scriptures, Romans 10:9, 10, were written by Paul to **saints**, to people who were **already** saved, to those who **already** had faith in Christ as their Lord and Savior.

Romans 1:7, 8, 11, 12

To all that be in Rome, beloved of God, called to be saints: Grace to you and peace from God our Father, and the Lord Jesus Christ. First, I thank my God through Jesus Christ for you all, that your faith is spoken of throughout the whole world. (11) For I long to see you, that I may impart unto you some spiritual gift, to the end ye may be established; (12) That is, that I may be comforted together with you by the mutual faith both of you and me.

Notes

We see then, that the book of Romans was not written to convert sinners, but to strengthen and establish believers, those who are already converted from their sins. New converts and disciples of Christ had been made during the Acts of the Apostles, during the establishment of the New Testament church. The epistles, Romans through Revelation, were written to solidify, establish, and promote the spiritual growth of both believers and new converts. These epistles do not show the way of salvation, they show individuals how to maintain and progress in their salvation.

Look at Romans 10:9, 10 in the Amplified Bible.

Amplified Bible: Romans10:9, 10

Because if you acknowledge and confess with your lips that Jesus is Lord and in your heart believe (adhere to, trust in, and rely on the truth) that God raised Him from the dead, you will be saved. For with the heart a person believes (adheres to, trusts in, and relies on Christ) and so is justified (declared righteous, acceptable to God), and with the mouth he confesses (declares openly and speaks out freely his faith) and confirms [his] salvation. AMP

Notes

The Amplified Bible expounds on the fact that a person who openly speaks forth (confesses) that Christ is his Lord, and truly believes within the depths of his heart that God raised Jesus Christ from the dead, that person is accepted by God because he is showing, or proving, that he is not ashamed to call Christ his Lord. He speaks aloud his faith in Christ that he is right *now* enjoying.

<u>Notes</u>

Paul records in Romans, chapters 9-11, that his heart breaks due to the refusal of his brethren and kinsmen (Israel) to submit to the righteousness of God, to confess Christ as their Redeemer. For the most part, the scribes, Pharisees, Sadducees, high priests, and the who's who of Israel, refused to confess Christ and threatened those who did confess Him.

John 9:22

These words spake his parents, because they feared the Jews: for the Jews had agreed already, that if any man did confess that he was Christ, he should be put out of the synagogue.

John 12:42, 43

Nevertheless among the chief rulers also many believed on him; but because of the Pharisees they did not confess him, lest they should be put out of the synagogue: For they loved the praise of men more than the praise of God.

<u>Notes</u>

Jesus is adamant about being acknowledged in the lives of His people. The sacrifice of Jesus on the cross for the salvation of mankind was not done in secret. Secret followers do not bring Him glory.

Matthew 10:32, 33

Whosoever therefore shall confess me before men, him will I confess also before my Father which is in heaven. But whosoever shall deny me before men, him will I also deny before my Father which is in heaven.

Notes

It will eventually be known what a person truly believes "for out of the abundance of the heart the mouth speaketh." Matthew 12:34b . And just because someone *verbally* says that he/she is a follower of Christ does not make that confession true. The mouth and the heart have to be in complete agreement.

Let's revisit Acts 8 to prove how confession alone does not bring salvation. The eunuch **believed** and **confessed** that Jesus Christ was the Son of God. Yet, he, through Philip's teaching, was gladly baptized in water even after the eunuch confessed with his mouth the Lordship of Christ. Salvation is therefore not automatically possessed just by saying a few sentences aloud. When a soul "believeth unto righteousness", actions will show forth that belief.

The disciples of Jesus certainly believed that He was raised from the dead. They walked, talked, and ate with the resurrected Christ.

Luke 24:36-40

And as they thus spake, Jesus himself stood in the midst of them, and saith unto them, Peace be unto you. But they were terrified and affrighted, and supposed that they had seen a spirit. And he said unto them, Why are ye troubled? And why do thoughts arise in your hearts? Behold my hands and my feet, that it is I myself: handle me, and see; for a spirit hath not flesh and bones, as ye see me have. And when he had thus spoken, he shewed them his hands and his feet.

Notes

Jesus continued to teach his disciples after His resurrection from the dead. Before he ascended into heaven, he instructed them once more. "And, behold, I send the promise of my Father upon you: but tarry ye in the city of Jerusalem, until ye be endued with power from on high." Luke 24:49 . We see here that although the disciples had proof that Jesus was raised from the dead, they were still instructed to receive the Holy Ghost. This not only gave them power to perform miracles; the Holy Ghost enabled the disciples to endure the persecution that came their way because of their faith in Christ Jesus.

Finally, a mere confession of Christ does not secure salvation; true salvation is **confirmed** with and by a confession.

READER'S NOTES

_____

_____

_____

_____

_____

_____

_____

_____

_____

_____

_____

_____

_____

_____

_____

_____

_____

_____

_____

_____

_____

_____

_____

_____

_____

AFTERLIFE

Major Area #7

The Lives Of Men Cannot Be Sustained By Bread Alone.

Scriptures

Matthew 4:1-4

Then was Jesus led up of the Spirit into the wilderness to be tempted of the devil. And when he had fasted forty days and forty nights, he was afterward an hungred. And when the tempter came to him, he said, If thou be the Son of God, command that these stones be made bread. But he answered and said, It is written, Man shall not live by bread alone, but by every word that proceedeth out of the mouth of God.

John 6:26, 27

Jesus answered them and said, Verily, verily, I say unto you, Ye seek me, not because ye saw the miracles, but because ye did eat of the loaves, and were filled. Labour not for the meat which perisheth, but for that meat which endureth unto everlasting life, which the Son of man shall give unto you: for him hath God the Father sealed.

Deuteronomy 8:3

And he humbled thee, and suffered thee to hunger, and fed thee with manna, which thou knewest not, neither did thy fathers know; that he might make thee know that man doth not live by bread only, but by every word that proceedeth out of the mouth of the Lord doth man live.

Notes

The above scriptures explain why the world is experiencing and suffering with horrendous crimes, political corruption, racial discrimination, poverty, adultery, fornication, perversion, the list goes on and on and on......... The majority of the world's population is living *only* on the fuel of food: steaks, pork chops, chicken, potatoes, corn, pasta, and other favorite food staples. This is only existing, not living.

When the hearts of men do not seek the heart of God, chaos, disorder, and lawlessness rule everywhere. The written, preached, and taught Word of God is the design by which we are to design our lives. Since people have failed to live upright and godly lives according to the instructions in God's Word, mass shootings; serial killers; suicides; insensitive, uncaring children and teens; bullying and harassment; and obscene entertainment have been on a steady rise, causing billions of people to be unprepared to meet Jesus Christ at His imminent return.

2 Timothy 3:1-5

This know also, that in the last days perilous times shall come. For men shall be lovers of their own selves, covetous, boasters, proud, blasphemers, disobedient to parents, unthankful, unholy, Without natural affection, trucebreakers, false accusers, incontinent, fierce, despisers of those that are good, Traitors, heady, highminded, lovers of pleasures more than lovers of God; Having a form of godliness, but denying the power thereof: from such turn away.

Notes

The Word of God is the Word from God's mouth. Through His Word, God instructs human beings how to live their best lives. When men and women opt not to order their lives according to what is written in the Word of God and fail to teach their children to do the same, the words of Jesus are then fulfilled: men are living "by bread alone".

When we live by food (bread) only, we live within, and depend on, our own strength and direction. That's a recipe for disaster!

And food is not the only thing by which the world tries to sustain itself. Trust and false hopes are placed in countless venues of entertainment, accomplishments, education, travel, and a constant pursuit of [some kind of] discovery. While these things are used to enhance the enjoyment of earthly life, they cannot *be* your life.

Luke 12:15

And he said unto them, Take heed, and beware of covetousness: for a man's life consisteth not in the abundance of the things which he possesseth.

Notes

An "oldness", a stale routine, or boredom will set in when everything that is supposed to be pleasurable is not tempered with the wisdom and knowledge that is found within the Word of God. "It is the spirit that quickeneth; the flesh profiteth nothing: the words that I speak unto you, they are spirit, and they are life." John 6:63. A life with God at the helm is the only kind of life worth living.

Jeremiah 10:23

O Lord, I know that the way of man is not in himself: it is not in man that walketh to direct his steps.

Proverbs 3:5-8

Trust in the Lord with all thine heart; and lean not unto thine own understanding. In all thy ways acknowledge him, and he shall direct thy paths. Be not wise in thine own eyes: fear the Lord, and depart from evil. It shall be health to thy navel, and marrow to thy bones.

Psalms 119:9, 11, 105, 133

Wherewithal shall a young man cleanse his way? By taking heed thereto according to thy word. (11) Thy word have I hid in mine heart, that I might not sin against thee. (105)Thy word is a lamp unto my feet, and a light unto my path. (133) Order my steps in thy word: and let not any iniquity have dominion over me.

Notes

The entire chapter of Psalms 119 makes reference to the Word of God. Heaven is an impossible goal for anyone who tries to live his/her life without obedience to the Bible. It is not an antiquated, outdated Book, but a very relevant map of the beginning, middle, and end of this current, earthly life for all of humanity.

The Bible does not teach you how to fix other people. It teaches you how to fix *you*. A deliberate and diligent effort must be made to read and study the Word of God; spiritual growth and personal growth come as the

Word of God is consistently planted in the heart. Yes, Sunday sermons, Sunday school lessons, and Bible classes at the local church are needed, but your private study of God's Word is how real and steady growth will take place in your heart and, subsequently, in your life.

Notes

Along with prayer, the Word of God (Bible) is the route through which you will build a personal relationship with God. The Bible answers many of the questions we ask the Lord in prayer. And God's Word is how we maintain our spiritual equilibrium even as we continue to grow through His Word. Even after you obey the three steps of salvation that is found in Acts 2:38, [repentance, water baptism in the Name of Jesus Christ, and receiving the gift of the Holy Ghost], adhering to God's Word will be your life's blood. Feeding on the Word of God is how you continue in your salvation. Read it, study it, meditate on it, obey it, get to know God through it, and reap a glorious afterlife because of it: The Word of God!

Revelation 22:12

And, behold, I come quickly; and my reward is with me, to give every man according as his work shall be.

Notes

Everything in this Holy Ghost assigned book points to one major truth. **"Follow peace with all men, and holiness, without which no man shall see the Lord."** Hebrews 12:14 .

THE BONUS!
THE REVELATION

Whenever you become disillusioned with life in this present world, and you definitely will, (everyone eventually does), it will then be time for you to receive the deepest revelation, to decipher the world's oldest mystery, to understand and to accept the final, unadulterated truth.

What is it?

That <u>God Himself</u>, **IS**, and was always supposed to be:

Your **strongest passion**
Your **most ambitious goal**
Your **greatest mission**
Your **highest ministry**
Your **fervent pursuit**
Your **all consuming love**
Your **life's purpose**

<u>God Himself</u> is the *meaning* of life! **M**ystery **S**olved!

READER'S NOTES

THE AFTERLIFE

ABOUT THE AUTHOR

Ms. Fields is an ordained teaching evangelist. God placed a call on her life to teach people how to successfully transition from this life to the next life. Saved over 27 years, the author has served faithfully in the Church starting from the humble position of church janitor to the gracious role of poet laureate.

The Holy Spirit persistently prompted Evangelist Fields, already a writer and an author, to help others explore more fully the necessity of authentic Bible Salvation. The publication of The Afterlife is the result of His prompting.

Ms. Fields, to whom God has also given the gift of exhortation according to Romans 12:8, happily resides in Mississippi. She is available to speak at conferences, seminars, workshops, and other events.

Printed in the United States
By Bookmasters